凍凍果

凍凍果

凍凍果

ICY FRUIT

HOW MY GRANDFATHER SPREAD THE JOY OF ICE POPS ACROSS TAIWAN

凍凍果

written by
Charlotte Cheng

illustrated by
Vivian Mineker

Rocky Pond Books

My grandfather Agong always carried a well-worn bag of coins that would rustle in his pocket.

That bag, with a few simple words, carried a story of joyful jingles, sultry summers, and fresh frozen fruit, which began in 1965 in the lush valleys and mountains of an island called Taiwan.

There, Agong stood in an empty freezer,
where his breath turned to mist. The city
had changed and so had his business.
People no longer needed the pork he had to sell.

Agong kept wondering: What do I do with
an empty freezer? What else could I sell?

His mind wandered, until he thought of the hot and humid summer, when hardworking people often searched for a refreshing break.

At last, he had an idea.

So he traveled across the island and spoke to the farmers who labored in the fields.

There, they gathered juicy dragon's eye and crunchy star fruit. They plucked sweet guava and spiky pineapple that were loaded onto a train …

...which then rumbled into the hustle and bustle of Taipei.

There, in a kitchen, when the fruit finally arrived, Agong worked with cooks to peel the bumpy dragon's eye and chop the luscious guava—to mash chunks of the pineapple and blend slices of the star fruit with sprinkles of sugar.

There, in the freezer, Agong experimented.
After struggling with standard popsicle sticks,
he tried clear plastic bags made for tiny hands.

The fruit pouches gleamed like jewels in red, white, and yellow as they quickly turned to scrumptious fruit pops.

There, in the busy streets, Agong saw how food carts were often unnoticed as their jangling bells were drowned out by the honks of cars and scooters whizzing by.

And so, Agong organized a competition for composers. He asked them to write a joyful jingle about his tasty frozen treats.

He picked the best version and hired musicians to record the song, which would cut through the rumbling noise of Taipei.

Finally, Agong loaded a bike full of ice-cold fruit pops, and the rider played that cheerful tune while wandering through the city:

凍凍果

DELICIOUS, DELICIOUS ICY FRUIT
GATHER ROUND FOR ICY FRUIT!
REFRESHING, NUTRITIOUS, AND FLAVORFUL
GATHER ROUND FOR ICY FRUIT!

There, in the alleys, the bike would stop so people could gather in the sticky heat.

Toddlers nibbled bites of icy pineapple. Giggling kids slurped cold guava and star fruit. Grateful grown ups took time to enjoy a reviving treat.

And there, in the heart of Taipei, Agong turned one bike into many bikes that spread the joy of fruit pops across the city.

Then, over the span of five years, his icy fruit spread across the island while the music played through radios, televisions, and the hums of an entire generation.

Decades later, our family gathered to say goodbye to my grandfather, my Agong.

There, with friends from near and far, thousands of miles away from Taipei, three generations sang the music of fruit pops one final time.

DELICIOUS, DELICIOUS ICY FRUIT
GATHER ROUND FOR ICY FRUIT!
REFRESHING, NUTRITIOUS, AND FLAVORFUL
GATHER ROUND FOR ICY FRUIT!

Each time the melody echoes in my mind, Agong is there and so is his story . . . of joyful jingles, sultry summers, and fresh frozen fruit.

To my Agong, whose creative risks included imported souvenirs, flashy musical acts, frozen pork, and fruit pops.

Your passion and ingenuity are always with me. — C.C.

To all my family and friends in Taiwan: You inspired and illuminated every page of this book. — V.M.

Rocky Pond Books
An imprint of Penguin Random House LLC
1745 Broadway, New York, New York 10019

First published in the United States of America by Rocky Pond Books, an imprint of Penguin Random House LLC, 2025

Text copyright © 2025 by Charlotte Cheng
Illustrations copyright © 2025 by Vivian Mineker

Library of Congress Cataloging-in-Publication Data is available.

Manufactured in India · MAN · ISBN 9780593617755 · 10 9 8 7 6 5 4 3 2 1

Design by Cerise Steel · Text set in Isidora

The art was created digitally.